Carter G. Woodson

The Father of Black History

Patricia and Fredrick McKissack

Illustrated by Ned O.

❖ *Great African Americans Series* ❖

ENSLOW PUBLISHERS, INC.

44 Fadem Road	P.O. Box 38
Box 699	Aldershot
Springfield, N.J. 07081	Hants GU12 6BP
U.S.A.	U.K.

To Barbara, T.J., and C.C.

Library of Congress Cataloging-in-Publication Data

McKissack, Pat , 1944-
    Carter G. Woodson: the father of black history/ Patricia and
Fredrick McKissack : illustrated by Ned O.
       p. cm. — (Great African Americans Series)
    Includes Index.
    Summary: Simple text and illustrations describe the life and
accomplishments of the man who first pioneered the study of black
history.
    ISBN 0-89490-309-8
    1. Woodson, Carter Godwin, 1875–1950—Juvenile literature.
2. Historians—United States—Biography—Juvenile literature.
3. Afro-Americans—Historiography—Juvenile literature.
[1. Woodson, Carter Godwin, 1875–1950. 2. Educators.
3. Historians. 4. Afro-Americans—Biography.] I. McKissack,
Fredrick. II. Ostendorf, Edward, ill. III. Title. IV. Series:
McKissack, Pat, 1944- Great African Americans series.
E175.5.W65M35 1991
973'.049607302—dc20
[B]
                                        91-8813
                                        CIP
                                        AC

Printed in the United States of America

10 9 8 7 6 5 4

Photo Credits: Library of Congress, Prints & Photographs Division, p. 16; Moorland-Spingarn Research Center, Howard University, pp. 4, 14; Bill Rice, p. 27; National Archives, p. 24; St. Louis Public Library, p. 26; United States Postal Service, p. 28; West Virginia State Archives, p. 10.

Illustration Credits: Ned O., pp. 6, 7, 8, 11, 12, 17, 18, 19, 22.
Cover Illustration: Ned O.

Contents

Carter G. Woodson
Born: December 19, 1875, New Canton, Virginia.
Died: April 3, 1950, Washington, D.C.

1

Family Stories

The first history lessons Carter learned were about his own family. His mother, Anne Eliza Riddle, was born a **slave**.* She told stories about her life.

Carter's father told him stories, too. James Henry Woodson was also born a slave. His **master** beat him all the time.

One day James took the whip away

* Words in **bold type** are explained in *Words to Know* on page 30.

from his master and beat him with it. A group of men came to kill James. But he ran and hid in the woods for many, many days.

It was near the end of the **Civil War**. Soldiers from the North were in Virginia. They found James in the woods. They told him he was free. James became a soldier in the **Union Army**.

The war ended in April 1865. Soon after, James and Anne met and married. They moved to Huntington, West Virginia.

In 1874 they moved back to New Canton, Virginia. They bought a small farm. Carter was born there on December 19, 1875.

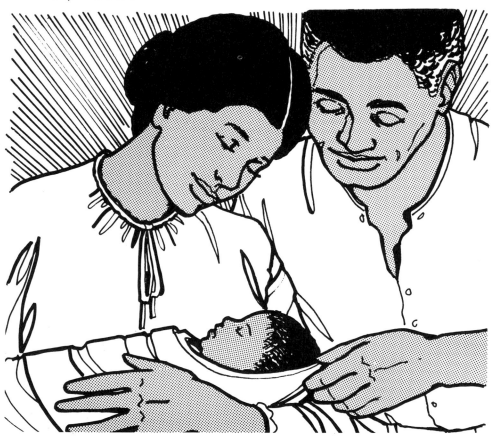

2

Never Too Late to Learn

Carter's father couldn't read or write. But, he always told his seven children, "It is never too late to learn."

Carter had to help work on the family farm. There wasn't much time for school. Still he learned how to read. He read every day.

When Carter was sixteen years old, he went to West Virginia with his older brothers. There he worked on the railroad and in a **coal mine**.

By 1893 Anne and James had moved back to Huntington, West Virginia. Carter had two younger sisters. They wanted to go to Douglass High School. Carter wanted to go there, too.

But he was eighteen years old. "It is never too late to learn," he told the **principal**.

The main street of Huntington, West Virginia in the early 1900s.

Carter had learned a lot on his own. He did very well on a test. So they let Carter start at Douglass High School. Then he surprised everyone when he **graduated** eighteen months later.

Next Carter went to **college**. After a few

months, he was asked to be the principal of a school. He took the job for two years. In the summers, he went to school.

In 1900 Carter was asked to be the principal of Douglass High School back in Huntington. He was proud to take the job. He stayed there three years.

Carter read every day. He tried to learn something new every day. He read to his students. And he told them, "It is never too late to learn."

Carter Woodson was a fancy dresser. He was also very good-looking. But, he never married. His friends wondered why. Dr. Woodson answered, "It wasn't because I didn't ask."

3

"Shake the Lomboy Tree"

On August 31, 1903, a letter came for Carter. He had been asked to come teach in the **Philippine Islands**. His work began on December 19, 1903.

Something was wrong. The children weren't learning. They didn't like to read. The other teachers said the children were lazy. Or their mothers and fathers didn't care. Carter wouldn't stop trying.

One day he sang a song for his students: "Come Shake the Apple Tree." But apples don't grow in the Philippines! So, Carter changed the words to "Come Shake the **Lomboy** Tree." The lomboy is a kind of plum. The children loved the song. They wanted to learn it. And they did.

Carter learned Spanish. He taught the

School children in front of their classroom in the Philippines in the early 1900s.

children about their own history and **heroes**. The children were proud of who they were. Soon they were reading and learning quickly.

After that, Carter put away the books. They were written for American children.

Carter thought about the school books back home. They didn't have much black history in them. Carter wrote home. "It is time to 'Come Shake the Lomboy Tree' in American schools."

THE JOURNAL

OF

NEGRO HISTORY

CARTER G. WOODSON
EDITOR

VOLUME I

1916

THE ASSOCIATION FOR THE STUDY OF NEGRO LIFE
AND HISTORY, Inc.
LANCASTER, PA., AND WASHINGTON, D. C.
1916

Dr. Carter Woodson wrote many books and articles. This was the first volume of *The Journal of Negro History*.

4

Teach Ourselves

Each summer Carter came home. He studied history at the University of Chicago. He came home for good in 1908. He needed to learn more. So he went to the University of Chicago. He graduated in March. He continued his studies and earned a higher **degree** in August of that same year!

Then Woodson went to Harvard University in Massachusetts. There he worked on the highest degree a student can earn—a **Ph.D.** He received his Ph.D. in history in 1912.

Dr. Woodson took a job at M Street High School in **Washington, D.C.** There he taught history, French, and Spanish.

History books still didn't have much about black people in them. "We must

teach ourselves," he said. At his school, black history was taught.

In 1914 Carter became a member of the **American Negro Academy**. The group found and saved African-American writings. They also tried to show that black people had done important things in history.

Dr. Woodson started the **Association for the Study of Negro Life and History** in 1915. "We will teach ourselves about ourselves," he said.

Carter Woodson wrote *The Miseducation of the Negro* in 1933. It showed the poor way African-American children were taught in school.

5

Be Proud

Most school children didn't know about the important things black people had done. Dr. Woodson wrote about these great African Americans.

Dr. Woodson had an idea that would help people learn more about black history.

Two of Dr. Woodson's heroes were Frederick Douglass and Abraham Lincoln. Douglass fought against slavery. And

Lincoln freed the slaves. Both men were born in February.

In February 1926 Dr. Woodson planned the first "Negro History Week" program. It was the start of what is now called Black History Month.

Dr. Woodson studied and wrote about **Africa**, too. He wanted black people to

THIRTY-FIRST ANNUAL CELEBRATION OF
NEGRO HISTORY WEEK
FEBRUARY 12-19, 1956

THE ASSOCIATION FOR THE STUDY OF NEGRO LIFE AND HISTORY
1538 NINTH STREET, Northwest, WASHINGTON 1, D. C.
Founded by Carter G. Woodson (1875-1950)

Since the 1920s black history programs like this one have been held all over the country.

know about their African **ancestors**.
"Africa has a great past," he told school
children all over the country. "Be proud!"

Dr. Woodson stopped teaching to run
the association full-time. He never

The center house was where the Association for the Study of
Negro Life and History started. Carter Woodson lived above
the office until he died.

The United States post office issued a stamp honoring Carter G. Woodson in 1984.

married. He lived over the association's office in a small apartment. He was a neat man who liked nice clothes. He was always busy, but he was hardly ever late.

On April 3, 1950, Dr. Woodson was late for work. Something had to be wrong. And it was. He had died during the night.

Dr. Woodson's work helped show the world that African Americans had much to be proud about. Today his work goes on.

Words to Know

Africa—The second largest continent in the world.

American Negro Academy—An organization that found and saved African-American writings.

ancestors—People who lived long ago, but are related by family or race.

Association for the Study of Negro Life and History—An organization started to teach black people about themselves and their history.

Civil War—A war fought within one country. In the United States, the Civil War was fought between the states in the North and South.

coal mine—A mine is a place in the ground where minerals—like coal, gold, and silver—are dug out.

college—A school beyond high school.

degree—A signed piece of paper that a college or university gives a person when he or she has graduated.

graduate (GRAJ-uh-wait)—To finish all the studies at a school.

hero—A person who is looked up to because of the things he or she does.

lomboy tree—A plum tree that grows in the Philippine Islands.

master—A ruler or a person who controls another. Someone who owns a slave is called a master.

Ph.D.—The highest degree a student can get from a university. It means doctor of philosophy.

Philippine Islands—A group of small islands in the South Pacific Ocean.

principal—The head of a school.

slave—A person who is owned by another. That person can be bought or sold.

Union Army—The army that fought for the North in the Civil War.

Washington, D.C.—The place where the United States capital is located. D.C. stands for District of Columbia.

Index